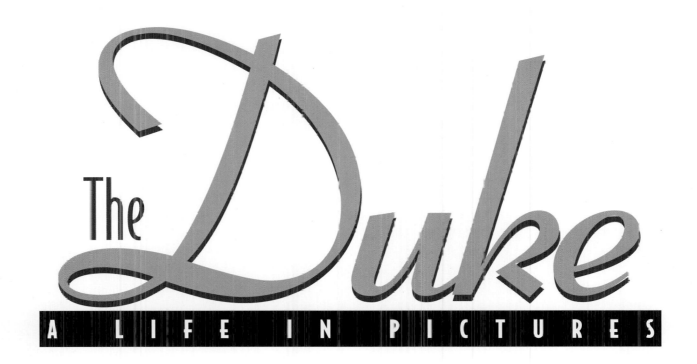

The Duke
A LIFE IN PICTURES

The Duke

A LIFE IN PICTURES

Rob L. Wagner

MetroBooks

MetroBooks

An Imprint of Friedman/Fairfax Publishers

Library of Congress Cataloging-in-Publication Data

Wagner, Rob, 1954-
    The Duke: a life in pictures / Rob Leicester Wagner.
        p. cm.
    Includes bibliographical references and index.
    ISBN 1-56799-466-0 (hc)
    1. Wayne, John, 1907-1979—Portraits. 1. Title.
PN2287.W454W34   1997
791.43'028'092—dc21   97-13041
                                                                CIP

Editor: Stephen Slaybaugh
Art Director: Kevin Ullrich
Designers: Millie Sensat and Ruth Diamond
Photography Editor: Karen Barr

Color separations by Ocean Graphic International Company Ltd.
Printed in China by Leefung-Asco Printers Ltd.

5   7   9   10   8   6   4

For bulk purchases and special sales, please contact:
Friedman/Fairfax Publishers
Attention: Sales Department
15 West 26th Street
New York, NY 10010
212/685-6610   FAX 212/685-1307

Visit our website: http://www.metrobooks.com

Photography Credits

Archive Photos: pp. 11, 22 bottom right, 62 bottom, 87 left; ©Jack Albin: p. 52 bottom; Popperfoto: p. 20 top

Corbis-Bettmann: pp. 16, 20 bottom, 22 bottom left, 26-27, 27, 29 top, 30, 30-31, 43, 44 bottom, 50, 60 top, 66 bottom, 67 left, 67 top right, 77 top, 82, 84 bottom, 85 top

The Kobal Collection: pp. 2, 13, 19 top, 19 bottom, 21 top, 21 bottom, 23, 24, 29 bottom, 32, 33 right, 34, 35, 36, 37, 38, 40, 41, 42 bottom, 47, 56, 57, 58 top, 58 bottom, 59 top, 59 bottom, 60 bottom, 61, 62 top, 63 bottom, 64 bottom, 65 top, 66 top, 69 top, 69 bottom, 76 top, 85 bottom right, 86 top

Penguin/Corbis-Bettmann: pp. 15 top, 28 top, 39 bottom

Photofest: pp. 14 top, 15 bottom, 17, 18, 78 top, 78 bottom

Retna: Camera Press: pp. 70 top, 87 right; ©DOC. PELE/STILLS: pp. 8, 9, 10, 46 top, 48, 49, 68 top, 70 bottom, 76 bottom, 79, 91; ©Holland: pp. 6, 22 top, 28 bottom, 74 top

REX Features: LTD-London: pp. 46 bottom, 53 top; REX USA LTD.: pp. 83, 92

Springer/Corbis-Bettmann: pp. 12, 25, 33 left, 39 top, 42 top, 44 top, 45, 51, 53 bottom, 64 top, 65 bottom, 71, 74 bottom, 80-81, 89, 90

UPI/Corbis-Bettmann: pp. 14 Bottom, 52 top, 54 top, 54 bottom, 55, 63 top, 67 bottom right, 68 bottom, 72, 73 top, 73 bottom, 75 top, 75 bottom, 77 bottom, 84 top, 85 bottom left, 86 bottom, 88-89, 93

Dedication

In memory of Jesus "Chapo" Heredia

CONTENTS

Introduction

Above: Never a member of active military service, John Wayne always regretted that he had not had the opportunity to wear a uniform and serve his country during the war years, due to his contract obligations with Republic Pictures. But his contributions to the war effort in some of Hollywood's finest war films more than made up for any perceived shortcomings.

Opposite: Duke Morrison paid his dues as an actor, working on dozens of oaters on Poverty Row. Shoestring studios such as Mascot Monogram, and Republic gave him opportunities to work at his craft in the early days.

Duke and his third wife, Pilar Pallete, were married on November 1, 1954, in Hawaii.

There is probably no Hollywood actor who is so misunderstood or whose myth is so difficult to separate from reality, as John Wayne.

To identify John Wayne as an American icon has become a time-worn cliché. If anything, this label diminishes his body of work as an actor and obscures the reality of John Wayne the man.

Critics have often taken potshots at his acting ability, failing to understand that John Wayne was simply good at being John Wayne. His persona fit the roles he played. It can be argued that there is little distinction between Wayne playing Wayne, Clark Gable being Clark Gable, or Robert Redford playing Robert Redford.

But it was the variation of the John Wayne persona that made him a truly remarkable actor. Young and understanding in *Stagecoach* (1939); old, cynical, and unbending in *Red River* (1948); heroic and sacrificing in *Sands of Iwo Jima* (1949); and proud and patriotic in *The Green Berets* (1968), he drew on a wide range of emotions that painted a touching portrait of the man.

Born Marion Robert Morrison on May 26, 1907, in Winterset, Iowa, John Wayne spent most of his childhood in Palmdale, and Glendale, California. He played football at Glendale High School and later the University of Southern California. A surfing injury ended his budding sports career, but Tom Mix, the great western film

star of the 1920s, gave him a job moving furniture on film sets.

In 1926, Fox Studios director John Ford took a liking to Wayne, using him in a number of scenes that required little or no acting ability. It was the break that Wayne needed and he never looked back.

For a while it appeared that Wayne would be relegated to "B" and "C" pictures, slogging his way through serials at Mascot and Republic Pictures. But his breakthrough performance occurred when Gary Cooper rejected the part of Ringo Kid in *Stagecoach*. Ford, who was directing the film, offered the part to Wayne. It launched his career to a string of big pictures, ranging from *They Were Expendable* (1945) to the Ford cavalry trilogy of *Fort Apache* (1948), *She Wore a Yellow Ribbon* (1949), and *Rio Grande* (1950).

John Wayne's role in *The Shootist* (1976) has long been considered the quintessential farewell performance of an actor. He played a gunslinger—suffering from cancer and out of place in a burgeoning modern world—going out in a blaze of glory in a final gunfight that evoked pathos for the man, the actor and the character.

John Wayne died on June 11, 1979, from cancer. It's been our habit to pigeonhole him as a great western film star, but that would be unfair. His five decades of film work are perhaps unparalleled by any other film actor.

No other western film star captured the stoic dignity of a man standing up for his principles and ideals as well as John Wayne did.

Chapter One

From Oaters to Stardom

Above: Marion Morrison enjoyed great success on the University of Southern California football team, but, more important, it paved the way to his getting a job with silent western film star Tom Mix. Morrison's first job was moving furniture and props for the legendary actor.

Opposite: Marion Robert Morrison, circa 1911 with his younger brother, Robert. The boys' father, Clyde, was the only druggist in Winterset, Iowa. The family moved to California in 1913.

Right: Enjoying his first screen credit as Duke Morrison in Fox's *Words and Music* (1929), he played opposite Lois Moran under James Tingling's direction.

Below: Josephine Saenz and Duke were married in 1933. Wayne was fixed up with Josephine's sister, Carmen, on a blind date, but he fell in love with Josephine the first time he met her. The couple was married for twelve years.

Above: Duke joined director John Ford for their second picture together and Duke's third overall film in *Salute* (1929) at Fox. For the film, he used the screen name Duke Morrison; the film also starred Kenneth MacKenna and Frank Albertson (left).

Right: Always comfortable in a football uniform, Duke's early roles were no more than a walk-on or a face in the crowd. This time he's behind actor David Butler (holding the football) in a locker-room scene of an early film.

Armed with a big budget and top director Raoul Walsh, Fox's *The Big Trail* (1930) was Duke's first major film role. The inexperienced actor could not carry the film, and it flopped at the box office.

Now billed as John Wayne, he appeared opposite Virginia Cherrill in Fox's *Girls Demand Excitement* (1931). The year 1931 proved to be Duke's last year with Fox for decades: he would not make another film for the studio until 1958.

T*hree Girls Lost* (1931) was Wayne's last film for Fox after the debacle of *The Big Trail*. Here he plays opposite bright-eyed newcomer Loretta Young.

Left: Wayne posed for this still in 1933 for Monogram's *West of the Divide* (1934).

Below: The mid-1930s might be best described as Duke's lost years. He appeared in countless Poverty Row films. Here, he joins players in *'Neath Arizona Skies* (1934) for Monogram.

Right: Young and lean, Duke displays an intensity not found in many Poverty Row actors of the era.

Below: Duke managed to land a string of roles in western films for Warner Bros., such as *The Big Stampede* (1932) with Noah Beery (right).

Above: Wayne learned his craft in such forgettable films as *Rainbow Valley* (1934) for Monogram. In the film, he played an undercover government agent.

Left: *The Oregon Trail* (1936) was Duke's fourth film for Republic after the company was formed from several Poverty Row studios.

Left: Duke joined Claire Trevor in *Stagecoach* for his breakthrough role of Ringo Kid. The movie was directed by John Ford for producer Walter Wanger. Ford's highly disciplined, if not occasionally cruel, direction allowed Duke to give one of his finest performances.

Below, left: Ringo Kid, the epitome of chivalry. Wayne's character played against the grain of typical oaters by befriending and protecting Claire Trevor's character, a woman of loose morals.

Below, right: This publicity poster for *Stagecoach* displays Wayne sharing top billing with Claire Trevor.

Opposite: Wayne sits beside Andy Devine while George Bancroft, left, talks to a player. *Stagecoach*, scripted by Dudley Nichols, was tailor-made for Wayne.

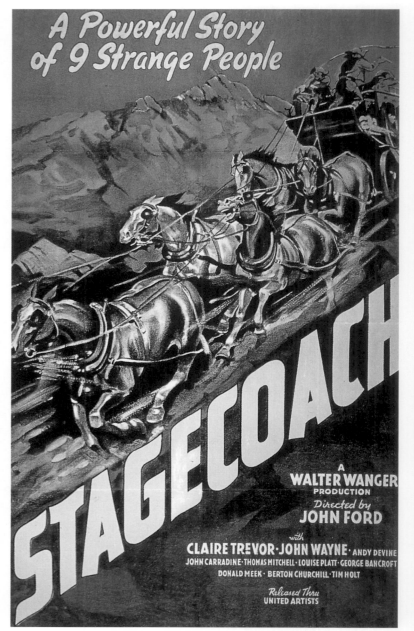

A Powerful Story of 9 Strange People

STAGECOACH

A WALTER WANGER PRODUCTION

Directed by JOHN FORD

with

CLAIRE TREVOR · JOHN WAYNE · ANDY DEVINE

JOHN CARRADINE · THOMAS MITCHELL · LOUISE PLATT · GEORGE BANCROFT

DONALD MEEK · BERTON CHURCHILL · TIM HOLT

Released Thru UNITED ARTISTS

oming off her success in *Destry Rides Again* (1939), Marlene Dietrich was offered any leading man she wanted for *Seven Sinners* (1940). She chose Wayne. An off-screen romance between the stars lasted three years.

Duke was reunited with director Raoul Walsh for the first time since the poorly received *The Big Trail*, this time for *Dark Command* (1940) with Claire Trevor and Walter Pidgeon. Wayne's success in *Stagecoach* provided him with meatier roles and top-quality productions.

Above: Handsome and confident, Duke emerged as a bona fide star appearing in Paramount's *Shepherd of the Hills* (1941), directed by Henry Hathaway.

Left: Looking a little uncomfortable in a top hat and tuxedo, Duke appears in Republic's *Lady From Louisiana* (1941), which costarred Ray Middleton and Ona Munson.

Right: After ending 1940 working for Walter Wanger in *The Long Voyage Home* and *Seven Sinners* for Universal, Duke returned to Republic to play opposite Frances Dee in *A Man Betrayed* (1941).

Below: Suave gentleman Ray Milland was cast opposite the rough-and-tumble Wayne, whose character ultimately gives his life to save Milland's in *Reap the Wild Wind*.

Above: *Three Faces West* (1940) demanded a broadening of Duke's acting range for his portrayal of a stubborn farmer. The film also starred Sigrid Gurie and Charles Coburn.

Left: Marlene Dietrich and Duke heat up the screen in *The Spoilers* (1942) under Ray Enright's direction for Universal.

Above: Republic's *In Old California* (1942) spurred the studio publicity mill to make much of Duke playing a druggist, his father's profession. He starred with Binnie Barnes, who played a dance hall girl.

Right: Duke was already an established star when he appeared in *In Old Oklahoma* (1943) for Republic. From left, Paul Fix, Albert Dekker, Duke, Gabby Hayes, and Martha Scott.

Marlene Dietrich joins Duke on a break from filming *Pittsburgh* (1942), by far the best of the three films that featured the pair.

Below: Never one to shy away from the physical side of acting, Duke tackles a bull. He preferred to perform many of his own stunts, even late in his career.

Above: Wayne prepares for a scene in Universal Pictures' *The Spoilers* (1942).

Chapter Two

The Duke at War

Above: Wayne shares a laugh with director David Miller on the set of *The Flying Tigers*. The 1942 film was the first of many patriotic military films he acted in.

Opposite: A quiet moment with Jean Arthur in *Lady Takes a Flyer* (1943), directed by William A. Seiter and produced by RKO Radio Pictures.

The *Flying Tigers* (1942) was actually a reworking of Howard Hawks' *Only Angels Have Wings* (1939), with Wayne cast in the Cary Grant part.

In Republic's 1944 hit, *The Fighting Seabees*, with Susan Hayward, Wayne's character, Wedge Donovan, dies for his country.

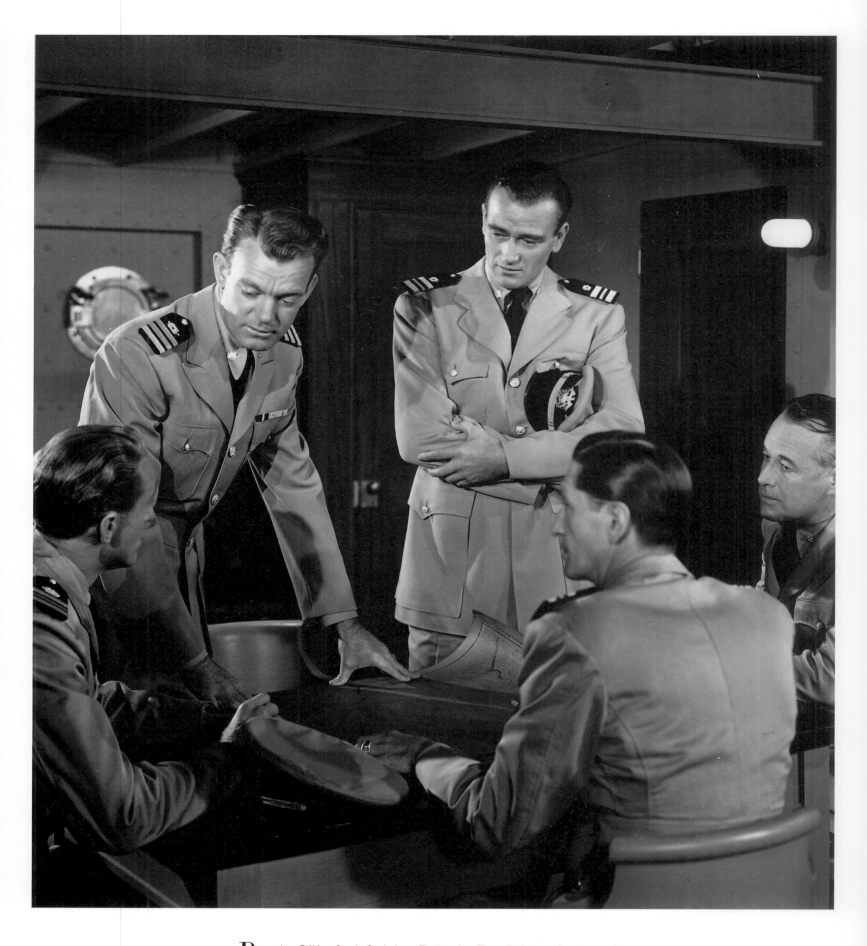

Dennis O'Keefe, left, joins Duke in *The Fighting Seabees* for Republic Pictures.

Right: Wayne plays a scene in *Back to Bataan* (1945). He and director Edward Dmytryk were often at odds on the set. Duke bristled at Dmytryk's jokes about patriotism. Dmytryk later was jailed for refusing to name suspected communist sympathizers in the film industry.

Below: Never a soldier in real life, Wayne convincingly storms a beach with his Filipino comrades in *Back to Bataan*. His string of war films during the 1940s cemented his reputation as a patriot and selfless hero with American audiences.

The U.S. government asked Wayne to star in *Back to Bataan* to boost troop morale. The RKO film starred Beulah Bondi, left, Richard Loe, and also featured Anthony Quinn and Paul Fix. Wayne plays an officer who leads a band of Filipino guerillas to victory in the South Pacific.

Perhaps one of Wayne's best war films was *They Were Expendable*, with Donna Reed and Robert Montgomery. During filming, Wayne divorced Josie and remained unhappy about not being able to join the military.

eft: Robert Montgomery, long a leading man in films, shares a scene with Duke in *They Were Expendable*. The film was based on the true story of the United States' PT boat squadron in the Philippinnes. Montgomery's second billing to Wayne demonstrated just how far Duke's star had risen.

pposite: Wayne played hard-driving, hard-drinking Marine sergeant John M. Stryker in *Sands of Iwo Jima* under the helm of Allan Dwan. His character's death by a sniper's bullet in the last reel stunned audiences. He was nominated for an Academy Award for his performance.

ight: Hitting the beach with John Agar in *Sands of Iwo Jima*. In his role as a Marine sergeant fighting in the invasion of the island, Duke essentially played the Everyman battling for honor in war.

Left: Duke confers with script supervisor Robert Walker, right, and supporting player Jay C. Flippin on the set of *Flying Leathernecks* (1951). Audiences rejected Duke's unsympathetic Marine fighter squadron commander who sends his men to a certain death.

Right: Duke is hoisted via breeches buoy from an aircraft carrier to a destroyer in the final scene of MGM's *The Wings of Eagles* (1957). Wayne played real-life commander Frank "Spig" Wead, one of the U.S. Navy's great modern heroes.

John Ford and Duke head the MGM cast and crew aboard the USS *Philippine Sea* for *The Wings of Eagles*.

Left: *Jet Pilot* (1957), starring Wayne and Janet Leigh, was a Howard Hughes production filmed in 1950 but not released until 1957 due to a variety of reasons but mostly as a result of Hughes' whimsical attitude towards filmmaking. It failed miserably at the box office thanks to Hughes' unintentional sabotage.

Right: John Wayne and Patricia Neal were teamed for Otto Preminger's blockbuster *In Harm's Way* (1965). The crew thought sparks would fly between Preminger, a strict disciplinarian, and Wayne, who always approached his craft more casually. The skeptics were wrong: the two got along very well. In the film, which once again takes place in the South Pacific during WWII, Wayne plays a naval officer.

Duke directs his crew for *The Green Berets*, a patriotic, if not controversial, depiction of the Vietnam War. It was panned by critics and flopped at the box office.

Left: Duke portrays Lt. Col. Ben Vandervort of the 82nd Airbourne Division in *The Longest Day* (1962).

Opposite: Filming *The Green Berets* at Fort Benning, Georgia, in 1967, Duke was determined to show support for American troops in Vietnam. He told his wife, Pilar, "Honey, somebody has to stand up for those guys."

Chapter Three

On the Home Front

Above: Although his schedule was hectic, John Wayne always took time to be with his children whenever possible. Here he plays leapfrog with Michael, 11 (on dad's shoulders); Melinda, 3 (front); Antonia, 5 (rear); and Patrick, 9 (second from rear).

Opposite: John Wayne with his second wife, Esperanza Baur. The couple met in early 1944 while Wayne was on a business trip to Mexico City. They were married on January 17, 1946, in Long Beach, California. Their marriage was rocky for many years and ended in divorce in 1954. Duke would marry Pilar Pallete only days later.

Above: Duke, with Richard Weldy and Weldy's then-wife, Pilar Pallete, in Tingo Maria in Lima, Peru. Pilar was estranged from Weldy at the time she met Duke. She later had her marriage annulled.

Right: Duke and Pilar share a moment at the Hollywood Roosevelt Hotel. Duke proposed to Pilar then immediately offered her a film contract.

Left: John Ethan Wayne joins his father on a film set. Pilar and Duke named Ethan after Ethan Edwards, the character portrayed by Duke in *The Searchers* (1956).

Below: Wayne adored his daughters Melinda, 14, left, and Tori, 18, but always felt guilty for not spending more time with them. The girls, however, felt very comfortable with their father.

Left: Wayne joins his son Pat, 15, on the set of *Mister Roberts* (1955), in which Pat had a part. At the time, Duke was filming *The Sea Chase* (1955).

Opposite: On breaks during the filming of *The Hellfighters* (1968), Duke gave his daughter Aissa riding lessons.

Right: Aissa Wayne was part of the cast of *The Alamo* (1960) and took direction from her father very well.

Chapter Four

Postwar Fame

A bove: Harry Carey, a longtime friend of Duke, shares a scene with Wayne and Gail Russell in *Angel and the Badman* (1947) for Republic. Carey, Paul Fix, Ward Bond, and Yakima Canutt were part of an informal stock company that played in Wayne films.

O pposite: Dame Judith Anderson (center) and Lorraine Day (right) filled out the cast in the non-western *Tycoon* (1947) for RKO Radio Pictures.

Left: From left, cameraman Archie Stout, producer-star Wayne, second unit director Yakima Canutt, and director James Edward Grant prepare for a scene in *Angel and the Badman*. In the film, Wayne plays a gunslinger who ultimately must choose between killing the man who murdered his foster-father or being with the woman he loves.

Right: Not only is there a lot of work in acting, but reading scripts is an undertaking too. Here, Duke prepares for *Angel and the Badman*.

Left: Gig Young appeared with Duke in *Wake of the Red Witch* (1949). Young stood well over six feet tall but looks considerably smaller beside his costar. Many actors were reluctant to appear opposite Wayne for that reason.

Below: *Red River* proved to be a milestone film for Duke, who solidified his acting credentials as the stubborn Tom Dunson. He had misgivings about playing opposite Montgomery Clift, right in his film debut. Clift projected fragility, not masculinity, but the screen chemistry was an inspired piece of casting by Howard Hawks. *Red River* is about a cattle owner (Wayne) who must drive his herd from Texas to Missouri as there is no market for the cattle in the impoverished South. Along the way his foster-son (Clift) deserts him and they lose control of the drive.

Right: The famous fistfight between Duke and Montgomery Clift in *Red River*. Playing opposite Clift, whose acting skills were superb, and under Howard Hawks' direction, Wayne later stated that it was the first time he felt like a real actor.

Below: In *3 Godfathers* (1949) Duke played a likable outlaw who stumbles into town with an orphaned infant following a hellish trek across the desert. For his troubles he is sent to prison for bank robbery. The John Ford film opened to mixed reviews but is now considered a Wayne classic.

ARG-62

The *Fighting Kentuckian* (1949) was a huge moneymaker for John Wayne, who produced the film for Republic. Directed by George Waggner, Duke appeared opposite Oliver Hardy in one of his rare dramatic roles.

Right: John Wayne portrays Captain Kirby York with Henry Fonda as Colonel Thursday in Ford's bravura *Fort Apache* for RKO. The film documents a colonel's attempt to win over his troops as well as leave a mark on military history.

Below: *She Wore a Yellow Ribbon* marked a change in Duke's career as he moved from romantic leads to older roles. Here he poses with (from left to right) Joanne Dru, John Agar, and Harry Carey, Jr.

Left: Ward Bond, left, and John Ford remained close friends and colleagues with Wayne for many decades.

Right: *Rio Grande*, with Maureen O'Hara, was the last of the Ford cavalry trilogy, which started with *Fort Apache* and was followed by *She Wore a Yellow Ribbon*. It was the weakest effort of the three.

Below: Duke pulls Maureen O'Hara close to him in *The Quiet Man* (1952), a film that featured four of Duke's children in the cast. The picture is the story of an American boxer who returns to his native Ireland and has difficulties with local customs as well as his love's brother.

Right: The big Irish galoot, as he was nicknamed while playing Sean Thornton, weds Maureen O'Hara in *The Quiet Man*.

Left: In perhaps his most ruthless role. Duke played Ethan Edwards, the Indian-hating man bent on finding his two nieces, who had been abducted by Comanches, in *The Searchers* (1956). Here, he shares a scene with Jeffrey Hunter.

Below: Ethan Edwards (John Wayne) and Martin Pawley (Jeffrey Hunter) pressure a Commanche woman for information on Edwards' abducted niece in *The Searchers*. Edwards' niece was played by Natalie Wood.

Left: Duke recruited veteran William Wellman to direct *Blood Alley* (1955) costarring Lauren Bacall. *Blood Alley* was the first film for his newly formed Batjac Productions.

Below: Wayne starred in the disappointing *The Sea Chase* (1955) with Lana Turner and David Farrar. *The Sea Chase*, while forgettable for audiences, was memorable to Duke and Pilar, who wed on location in Hawaii.

Right: In perhaps his most embarrassing movie—or possibly second to *The Barbarian and the Geisha* (1958)—Wayne leads the cast of the Dick Powell-directed *The Conqueror* (1956) for RKO.

Above: Duke attends a Hollywood charity event with Veronica Cooper, wife of Gary Cooper, to raise funds for mentally retarded children.

Right: Duke prepares to take flight for Italy to film *Legend of the Lost* (1957) with Sophia Loren.

Left: A scene with Sophia Loren in *Legend of the Lost*. The film was directed by Wayne's old reliable, Henry Hathaway.

Below: Sophia Loren takes a firearm lesson from the master at a shooting gallery in Rome. The pair had just completed location shooting for *Legend of the Lost*.

Above: The weight of the world was on Duke's shoulders as he produced and directed the larger-than-life *The Alamo* (1960). The epic film showcased Wayne's talents as a director, but stretched him thin as an actor. Although popular with audiences, it received mixed reviews by critics.

Left: Richard Widmark joins the *Alamo* cast as Jim Bowie. Duke had to mortgage his company, Batjac Productions, to finance the film.

Above: Duke took a change of pace from his feature, *The Alamo*, with the light-hearted adventure *North To Alaska* (1960), which also starred Capucine and Stewart Granger.

Left: While Duke made a living portraying men in the saddle, James Stewart turned to westerns in the 1950s to save his failing career. It worked. By the time Stewart appeared in *The Man Who Shot Liberty Valance* (1962) with Wayne, he was a veteran cowboy actor.

Lee Van Cleef (left) and Strother Martin (center) rounded out an all-star cast in the intelligent western, *The Man Who Shot Liberty Valance*. Duke complained good-naturedly that the rest of the cast all got juicy roles, leaving him with little to do with his character.

Duke takes Elizabeth Allen over his knee for a good spanking in
Donovan's Reef (1963) for Paramount.

Right: John Wayne is flanked by Lloyd Nolan and Claudia Cardinale in box seats for the first scene of *Circus World* (1964), which was shot on location in Barcelona. It was directed by Henry Hathaway and produced by Paramount.

Left: Duke leaving Los Angeles' Good Samaritan Hospital in 1964 with his wife, Pilar, following cancer surgery to remove his left lung. Up until he was diagnosed with cancer, he had smoked about five packs of cigarettes a day

Right, top: Produced by Batjac Productions for Universal, *The War Wagon* (1967) costarred Kirk Douglas (shown here) and Howard Keel.

Right, bottom: Kirk Douglas displays his six-shooter to Joanna Barens and Duke in a publicity still for *The War Wagon*. Directed by Burt Kennedy, the film met with mediocre results at the box office.

Left: Hat askew, Wayne finds himself on the floor following a barroom brawl scene in *El Dorado* (1967). Wayne was reunited with Howard Hawks for the Paramount Film, which cast Duke as a gunfighter who has come to help his sheriff buddy stop a range war.

Right: Dean Martin and Duke ham it up backstage at the 1967 Golden Globe Awards. Martin had appeared with Wayne two years earlier in *The Sons of Katie Elder* (1965).

Left: Robert Mitchum joined the cast of *El Dorado* as a drunken lawman. The film was directed by Howard Hawks and featured Duke as an older, perhaps less confident, gunslinger.

Below: Jim Hutton shared acting duties with Wayne in *The Hellfighters* (1968). The Universal picture, directed by Andrew V. Molaglen, also featured Katherine Ross and Bruce Cabot.

Above: Duke celebrates his forty years in motion pictures with, from left to right, Lee Marvin, Clint Eastwood, Rock Hudson, Fred MacMurray, Jimmy Stewart, Ernest Borgnine, Michael Caine, and Laurence Harvey

Right: Duke with his mentor and idol, John Ford, in 1971. Through the years Wayne always gave credit to Ford for his successful career in motion pictures.

Opposite: Wayne with one of his favorite leading ladies, Maureen O'Hara.

Left: John Ethan Wayne joins his dad on the set of *Big Jake* in 1971. The movie stars Duke as an old marshall who helps a fourteen year-old girl track down her father's killer.

Below: Patrick Wayne is on the receiving end of a roundhouse punch from his dad as Maureen O'Hara looks on in *Big Jake* (1971), a Batjac production directed by George Sherman.

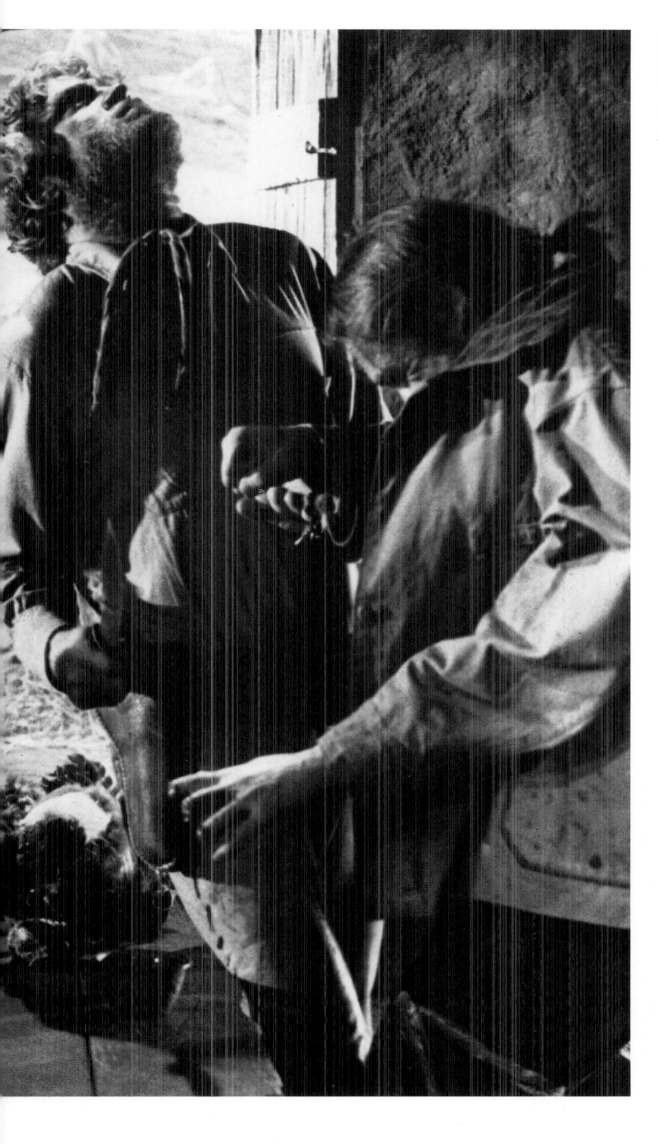

Chapter Five

Riding into the Sunset

Above: Following the removal of his left lung and two ribs in October 1964 for cancer, Duke started filming *The Sons of Katie Elder*. It was a tough shoot for the recovering actor. Director Henry Hathaway, always a tough taskmaster, believed that hard work would help his ailing friend.

Opposite: Barbra Streisand gives Duke a peck on the cheek backstage at the Academy Awards ceremonies, at which he won his Oscar for Best Actor for his performance as Rooster Cogburn in *True Grit*.

Left: Bob Hope gets a special guest star for the taping of the 1971 "Bob Hope Special" for NBC. Duke played a conservative father to Hope's hippie son in a skit.

Below: Duke fires off several rounds in a very physical scene in *The Train Robbers* (1973).

Left: A pair of grizzled veterans: Jackie Coogan shares a moment with the legendary cowpoke on the Warner Bros. lot in 1973 during a film break for *Cahill: United States Marshal*.

Above: Duke teamed up with Katharine Hepburn in *Rooster Cogburn* (1975). The good reception to the *True Grit* sequel was due in no small part to the chemistry between the two veteran actors.

Left: Wayne always had an interest in charities and children. In 1975, United Press International arranged for Carl Heart, 10, of Salina, Kansas, to meet his idol and get a trip to Disneyland. Heart was dying of leukemia.

Right: Wayne's last film, *The Shootist*, was steeped in irony as in it he portrayed a dying gunfighter preparing to end his life in a blaze of glory.

Below: Wayne with Ron Howard (now a director) in a scene from *The Shootist*.

Above: Portraying a man of quiet dignity in *The Shootist*, Duke was already sick with cancer. He had great difficulty during the shoot, tiring early and using oxygen tanks to help him breathe.

Right: The trademark hand across the stomach can't belie the fact that Duke looks tired following his second round of cancer surgery in 1979. This operation came just a year after Duke underwent successful open heart surgery.

Above: Wayne's handsome, rugged good looks were the envy of every man looking for a role model. Those looks, and his undeniable charisma, won him millions of admirers. A recent *People* magazine poll found John Wayne still ranked as one of the America's most popular film stars.

Left: A young Ricky Schroder greets a triumphant John Wayne, who returned from cancer surgery to present the Oscar for Best Picture for *The Deer Hunter* in April 1979.

Conclusion

He stood six feet four inches (193cm) tall, and was larger than life both on the screen and in person. He wore his patriotism on his sleeve and he has assumed the image of rugged individualism, much like America. Big. Gracious. Sentimental. Willful.

John Wayne loved his public and never forgot who put him on the pedestal as the country's most beloved actor. Just recently a new wire service poll emerged proclaiming Duke Wayne America's favorite actor—eighteen years after his death. And his complexity as a man and an actor is still fodder for film historians and cultural commentators alike.

The right-wing ideals Wayne's characters exhibited in *The Alamo* and *The Green Berets* were noted—and not infrequently lambasted—by critics, but he didn't feel the need to loudly defend his beliefs: John Wayne loved his country and made no apologies.

Perhaps part of it had to do with his never-realized dream of serving in the military. But more likely it was because he benefited greatly from a country willing to give him a chance. The door of opportunity cracked open for him ever so slightly when he was a young man and he leaped at the chance.

Wayne's father, Clyde, had found only failure on his farm in the Mojave Desert, followed by limited success as a druggist in Glendale, California, after the family moved there from Iowa. But despite his modest circumstances, the opportunities were there for the young Duke, who parlayed a respectable performance as a college football player into an acting career. Cowboy actor Tom Mix came around at just the right time to offer him a menial job moving furniture on the set of his films. And director John Ford was there at the right time to see a glint of talent behind that nervous, broad

Opposite: The growling, aging face of John Wayne as he portrays a cantankerous but kindly U.S. Marshal in *True Grit.*

Above: A classic portrait of John Wayne the man, the cowboy, and the legendary actor.

young face when he gave Duke a job as an extra. John Wayne combined these opportunities with hard work and was able to achieve a film career rivaled by few actors before or since.

"Patriot" was a label he wore proudly. Jane Fonda discovered that when she returned from Hanoi where she had posed for photographs with communist soldiers at the height of the protests against the Vietnam War and Duke refused to speak to her. And whether one agreed with his politics or not, John Wayne knew his stuff. Many bumbling souls made that discovery when they attempted to debate politics with him and found they weren't up to the task.

In her book, *John Wayne: My Life with the Duke*, Pilar Wayne recalled of her husband that he refused to allow antiwar protesters to get the best of him. In 1968, he left a Bob Hope show to raise scholarship funds for the University of Southern California. As he was leaving the building, he was greeted by three hundred protesters. Several people ran up to him and thrust a Vietcong flag in his face. Staring down at the young protesters and using his towering frame for effect, he said, "Please don't do that, fellows. I've seen too many kids your age wounded or dead because of that flag—so I don't take too kindly to it."

His words stunned the crowd. Then people burst into applause. In a volatile situation, Duke mustered quiet dignity to silence the critics.

Even as new polls list John Wayne as America's favorite actor, another battle over his image has emerged. Some historians take issue with his political beliefs and with the treatment of American Indians in his films.

These critics are blurring the lines between the private man and the public entertainer—as if entertainment and politics are one and the same. They aren't. As a performer, Duke played certain roles. As a private individual, he was entitled to his personal thoughts and opinions.

John Wayne's beliefs were simple and he lived by them. Work, and success will come. Respect your fellow man and you can count on him forever. To hell with the rest. It is that simple strength that shone through in his acting and imbued his roles with a sense of the heroic. And that's why he remains a legend today.

Opposite: The ravages of cancer took their toll on John Wayne: the old soldier faded away during his last years.

Below: Wayne's three sons and three daughters gather around a bust of the late actor in New York in 1982. From left to right are Melinda Muñoz, John Ethan, Toni LaCava, Patrick, Michael and Aissa Wayne.

Filmography

The Great K & A Train Robbery. Fox: 1926.

Brown of Harvard. Fox: 1926.

Bardelys the Magnificent. Fox: 1926.

The Drop Kick. Fox: 1927.

Annie Laurie. Fox: 1927.

Mother Machree. Fox: 1928.

Hangman's House. Fox: 1928.

Four Sons. Fox: 1928.

Words and Music. Fox: 1929.

Speakeasy. Fox: 1929.

Salute. Fox: 1929.

Noah's Ark. Fox: 1929.

The Forward Pass. Fox: 1929.

The Black Watch. Fox: 1929.

Rough Romance. Fox: 1930.

Men Without Women. Fox: 1930.

Cheer Up and Smile. Fox: 1930.

Born Reckless. Fox: 1930.

The Big Trail. Fox: 1930.

Three Girls Lost. Fox: 1931.

Range Feud. Columbia: 1931.

Men Are Like That. Columbia: 1931.

Maker of Men. Columbia: 1931.

Girls Demand Excitement. Fox: 1931.

The Deceiver. Columbia: 1931.

The Voice of Hollywood No. 13. Columbia: 1932.

Two-Fisted Law. Columbia: 1932.

That's My Boy. Columbia: 1932.

Texas Cyclone. Columbia: 1932.

Shadow of the Eagle. Mascot: 1932.

Ride Him Cowboy. Warner Bros.: 1932.

Lady and Gent. Paramount: 1932.

The Hurricane Express. Mascot: 1932.

Haunted Gold. Warner Bros.: 1932.

The Big Stampede. Warner Bros.: 1932.

The Three Musketeers. Mascot: 1933.

The Telegraph Trail. Warner Bros.: 1933.

Somewhere in Sonora. Warner Bros.: 1933.

Sagebrush Trail. Monogram: 1933.

Riders of Destiny. Monogram: 1933.

The Man from Monterey. Warner Bros.: 1933.

The Life of Jimmy Dolan. Warner Bros.: 1933.

His Private Secretary. Showmans Pictures: 1933.

College Coach. Warner Bros.: 1933.

Central Airport. First National: 1933.

Baby Face. Warner Bros.: 1933.

West of the Divide. Monogram: 1934.

The Trail Beyond. Monogram: 1934.

The Star Packer. Monogram: 1934.

Randy Rides Alone. Monogram: 1934.

The Man from Utah. Monogram: 1934.

The Lucky Texan. Monogram: 1934.

The Lawless Frontier. Monogram: 1934.

Blue Steel. Monogram: 1934.

'Neath the Arizona Skies. Monogram: 1934.

Westward Ho! Republic: 1935.

Texas Terror. Monogram: 1935.

Rainbow Valley. Monogram: 1935.

Paradise Canyon. Monogram: 1935.

The New Frontier. Republic: 1935.

Lawless Range. Republic: 1935.

The Desert Trail. Monogram: 1935.

The Dawn Rider. Monogram: 1935.

Winds of the Wasteland. Republic: 1936.

The Sea Spoilers. Universal: 1936.

The Oregon Trail. Republic: 1936.

The Lonely Trail. Republic: 1936.

The Lawless Nineties. Republic: 1936.

King of the Pecos. Republic: 1936.

Conflict. Universal: 1936.

Idol of the Crowds. Universal: 1937.

I Cover the War. Universal: 1937.

California Straight Ahead. Universal: 1937.

Born to the West. Paramount: 1937.

Adventure's End. Universal: 1937.

Santa Fe Stampede. Republic: 1938.

Red River Range. Republic: 1938.

Pals of the Saddle. Republic: 1938.

Overland Stage Raiders. Republic: 1938.

Wyoming Outlaw. Republic: 1939.

Three Texas Steers. Republic: 1939.

Stagecoach. United Artists: 1939.

The Night Riders. Republic: 1939.

New Frontier. Republic: 1939.

Allegheny Uprising. RKO: 1939.

Three Faces West. Republic: 1940.

Seven Sinners. Universal: 1940.

The Long Voyage Home. United Artists: 1940.

The Dark Command. Republic: 1940.

A Man Betrayed. Republic: 1941.

Lady from Louisiana. Republic: 1941.

Lady for a Night. Republic: 1941.

The Spoilers. Universal: 1942.

Reunion in France. MGM: 1942.

Reap the Wild Wind. Paramount: 1942.

Pittsburgh. Universal: 1942.

In Old California. Republic: 1942.

The Flying Tigers. Republic: 1942.

A Lady Takes a Chance. RKO: 1943.

In Old Oklahoma. Republic: 1943.

Tall in the Saddle. RKO: 1944.

The Fighting Seabees. Republic: 1944.

They Were Expendable. MGM: 1945.

Flame of the Barbary Coast. Republic: 1945.

Dakota. Republic: 1945.

Back to Bataan. RKO: 1945.

Without Reservations. RKO: 1946.

Desert Command. Republic: 1946.

Tycoon. RKO: 1947.

Angel and the Badman. Republic: 1947.

Wake of the Red Witch. Republic: 1947.

Red River. United Artists: 1948.

Fort Apache. RKO: 1948.

3 Godfathers. MGM: 1948.

She Wore a Yellow Ribbon. RKO: 1949.

Sands of Iwo Jima. Republic: 1949.

The Fighting Kentuckian. Republic: 1949.

Rio Grande. Republic: 1950

Operation Pacific. Warner Bros.: 1951.

Flying Leathernecks. RKO: 1951.

The Quiet Man. Republic: 1952.

Big Jim McLain. Warner Bros.: 1952.

Trouble Along the Way. Warner Bros.: 1953.

Island in the Sky. Warner Bros.: 1953.

Hondo. Warner Bros.: 1953.

The High and the Mighty. Warner Bros.: 1954.

The Sea Chase. Warner Bros.: 1955.

Blood Alley. Warner Bros.: 1955.

The Searchers. Warner Bros.: 1956.

The Conquerer. RKO: 1956.

The Wings of Eagles. MGM: 1957.

Legend of the Lost. United Artists: 1957.

Jet Pilot. RKO: 1957.

The Barbarian and the Geisha. Twentieth Century Fox: 1958.

Rio Bravo. Warner Bros.: 1959.

The Horse Soldiers. United Artists: 1959

North to Alaska. Twentieth Century Fox: 1960.

The Alamo. United Artists: 1960.

The Comancheros. Twentieth Century Fox: 1961.

The Man Who Shot Liberty Valance. Paramount: 1962.

The Longest Day. Twentieth Century Fox: 1962.

How the West Was Won. MGM: 1962.

Hatari! Paramount: 1962.

McLintock. United Artists: 1963.

Donovan's Reef. Paramount: 1963.

Circus World. Paramount: 1964.

The Sons of Katie Elder. Paramount: 1965.

In Harm's Way. Paramount: 1965.

The Greatest Story Ever Told. United Artists: 1965.

Cast a Giant Shadow. United Artists: 1966.

The War Wagon. Universal: 1967.

El Dorado. Paramount: 1967.

Hellfighters. Universal: 1968.

The Green Berets. Warner Bros.: 1968.

The Undefeated. Twentieth Century Fox: 1969.

True Grit. Paramount: 1969.

Rio Lobo. National General: 1970.

Chisum. Warner Bros.: 1970.

Big Jake. Batjac: 1971.

The Cowboys. Warner Bros.: 1972.

The Train Robbers. Warner Bros.: 1973.

Cahill: United States Marshal. Warner Bros.: 1973.

McQ. Warner Bros.: 1974.

Rooster Cogburn. Universal: 1975.

Brannigan. United Artists: 1975.

The Shootist. Paramount: 1976.

Bibliography

Bishop, George. *John Wayne: The Actor, The Man.* Thornwood, New York: Caroline House Publishers, 1979.

Carpozi, George, Jr. *The John Wayne Story.* New Rochelle, New York: Arlington House, 1972.

Wayne, Pilar, with Alex Thorleifson. *John Wayne: My Life with the Duke.* New York: McGraw-Hill, 1987.